The Sadness of Others

Books by Hayan Charara:

The Alchemist's Diary
The Sadness of Others

The Sadness of Others

Hayan Charara

Carnegie Mellon University Press
Pittsburgh 2006

ACKNOWLEDGMENTS

The poems in this book appeared in the following publications, often in their original form:

Anthology of Arab American and Diaspora Literature: "More Than We Dared," "The Price of Tomatoes," "To My Mother on the Occasion of the Fifth Year of Her Death"
Birmingham Poetry Review: "Walking the Dogs"
Connecticut Review: "English 101"
Hanging Loose: "Reacquaintance"
In Our Own Words: "More Than We Dared"
Mid-America Poetry Review: "Black Earth"
Photobetty: "Photography"
Poetry 30: Thirtysomething Thirtysomething American Poets: "Dog Poem," "Good Warm Up, Good Practice," "Washing My Father"
Poets Against the War: "The Price of Tomatoes"
Poets in their Thirties: "The Sadness of Others"
Present Tense: Poets In The World: "Here It Is," "More Than We Dared"
Roots & Culture: "Winter, Detroit"

My thanks to my friends whose insights and encouragement helped me to write these poems, especially to Thomas Fink, Douglas Goetsch, D.H. Melhem, Phyllis van Slyck, and Daniele Zavango.

Book design: Dylan Goings

The publication of this book is supported by a grant from the Pennsylvania Council on the Arts.

Library of Congress Control Number: 2005924485
ISBN- 13: 978-0-88748-445-2
ISBN- 10: 0-88748-445-X

10 9 8 7 6 5 4 3 2 1

PENNSYLVANIA
COUNCIL
ON THE
ARTS

CONTENTS

Good Warm Up, Good Practice / 9
Washing My Father / 11
Stepfather / 13
Photography / 14
Home / 15
The Size of Things / 18
Walking the Dogs / 20
Dog Poem / 21
Forgiveness / 23
The Sadness of Others / 24
My Best Days / 25
Job Interview / 26
Family Reunions / 27
Traffic / 29
Here It Is / 31
More Than We Dared / 33
The Price of Tomatoes / 35
Downtown / 37
Winter, Detroit / 38
There Were the Usual Reasons / 39
Falling Off the Bridge / 40
English 101 / 41
The Liturgy of Rain / 44
To My Ex-Wife / 45
Paperweight / 47
The Married Couple's Orchids / 48
Unfinished Business / 49
Reacquaintance / 50
To My Mother on the Occasion
    of the Fifth Year of Her Death / 51
Black Earth / 53
Changing the Subject / 54
The Rain / 56
The Last Thing / 57

for Rachel de Cordova

Either innocence is taken from you,
or you give it away.

—Chase Twichell

GOOD WARM UP, GOOD PRACTICE

I don't ever remember
burying a cat or dog.
I had them, they died.
A spot behind the garage,
a makeshift ditch
beside the dandelions,
or a cardboard box
wedged between
the week's trash—
these were the graves
of other people's pets.

Dino, my first mutt, ran away.
Someone else, I hope,
caressed his raggedy hair
and eased him into the ground.
My last dog—a black lab
that snarled more than
anything else, and also
lunged at my sister's face—
I'm sure was properly
disposed of by the same men
who put her to sleep.
There was the cat
I adopted from the Avon lady
who lived across the street.
A week after I picked him out
from a crowded litter box
and carried him home,
he disappeared.
I searched the neighborhood,
posted flyers on lampposts,
offered my allowance
as a finder's reward.
Finally my sister,
who was there, told me
the truth. Accidentally,
my mother had backed over him
while pulling out

of the drive. She scraped
the cat off the sidewalk,
threw the bag out
before I got home from school.

My good friend Angelo—
he has a wife,
is retired from the post office—
buried a cat when he was a kid.
Kitty. He dug a hole,
tucked her paws in,
placed a water bowl
and three pebbles
on a tiny mound.
He did the right thing.
"Good warm up, good practice."

I waited a year to visit
my mother's grave.
There, I forgot what to say.
I didn't bring flowers,
and when I rubbed
the etched letters of her name,
all I could muster
was the single word
each of my dead animals
must have been
sick and tired of hearing.
"No," I said. "No, no, no."

WASHING MY FATHER

His cupped hands hid the space
between his legs. Droplets,
which hung momentarily
at the lip of the faucet,
plopped into the tub—
the only noise in the bathroom.
Except for his breathing—
the deep inhales of steam
rising from the surface.
Except, too, the water
from a soapy sponge
pressed flat against his back—
the warm trickle
down his flanks.
I washed where
he could barely reach.

When he was ready,
I filled a jug with the bath water
he sat in, poured it over
the nape of his neck,
over his shoulders,
and lastly, over my hands.
I was careful not to dry them
with the towel hung on the knob—
this was his. Gently,
I locked the door behind me,
his back still turned away,
the click thunderous in that quiet.

This is not about pity.
I did not yet know that kind of love.
Nor is it about a son
bathing a father too old
to wash himself.
I was ten years old.
He was a young man.
Plain and simple,
my father made me.

It is what he did.
He never required a reason,
and nobody ever asked why.

STEPFATHER

She sleeps with an ear bent
toward the hallway, listening
for footsteps.
Her eyes watch the doorknob,
again, for a devastating click.
She begs the red hand
on the wall clock,
which pauses at each black dash
as if fearful of what
the next moment might bring,
to ignore the reckoning of time.
Eyelids heavy, she prays
for the dark to vanish
so that daybreak will bring relief.

At three A.M., I announce
my arrival, ease open
our bedroom door.
I am not necessarily polite
nor hardly inconsiderate of her sleep.
When she faces me, yawns,
and says, "It's late,"
I turn away.
I undress in the shadows, hesitant
to switch on the ceiling bulb.
It is not that I am embarrassed
or that I do not want her,
my wife, to watch me.
I unbuckle my belt in the dark
so that she is not
reminded.

PHOTOGRAPHY

An old photograph
taken near the conservatory
on Belle Isle,
the summer of 1976:
The father in his loose-
collared shirt lies next to his wife.
Beside them a boy sits
in the grass. If you must know
this was my family.
I could say we sat for hours
and watched birds near the pond
and leaning into the afternoon
we guessed at the names
of plants and broke twigs
off the trees in the park
to wish for enough light
to make the day last forever.
I could say that but it would be a lie.
The truth is I don't remember
what happened that day.
In the photograph
a boy smiles,
and as far as remembrance is
concerned,
there is a brief moment of happiness.
You must understand, however,
that in the course of a lifetime,
125th of a second
is no great matter at all.

HOME

for Doug Goetsch

It's been years since
the Irish priest
everyone suspected
as gay abandoned
the church on Calhoun.
It's been even longer
since the parish rectory
across the street
from Kresge's parking lot
closed its doors
and reopened
as a substance abuse center.
Summerland Restaurant
is now a coin laundromat,
the owner hauled off
to jail for stealing
tomatoes from the fruit market
next door. Hemlock Park
was never the same
after the City Council
posted signs to keep
non-residents out.
Fences weren't staked,
but there's talk of filling
the public pool
with cement. Warren Avenue
has a new name, either
"Little Lebanon"
or "Middle Eastern Market."
No one can agree,
and the Warren Boys
were all hired
for the assembly lines
at Ford Rouge.

No one made it
with Stephanie Flores.

A dollar short
for the cafeteria lunch
turned into late payments
on a thirty-year mortgage.

Permanent records
were never really
permanent.

The Beer & Wine
on Wyoming was reinvented
as a live poultry shop
and then a 99¢ store
and now it's empty.

You come here
on holidays,
spend the afternoons
with your father,
volunteer to take out
the trash or paint the garage.
You drive for hours
on singe-lane roads,
past storefronts,
alleyways, bus stops,
porches, backyards.
You park curbside
near the house
where your neighbor
screamed under
the clothesline pulley
and no one heard
and the only words
you can mouth are
"Once upon a time."

You can forgive
the past. Or you can
forget it or curse it.

Either way,
it doesn't matter.
Soon enough, you'll sleep
in another city,
dream of bridges
with different names,
and somehow even the air
that rises above
the sewer grates
will smell like lilacs
in spring. Meanwhile,
you try not to
run into old acquaintances,
and if you do
and they ask you
what you've been doing
with your life, you say
you're only visiting home,
you don't live here anymore.

THE SIZE OF THINGS

The molar cavity
I have made infamous
by claiming it is
the size of a marble
is in fact no larger
than a tomato seed.
And my dog,
a Jack Russell,
the most intelligent canine,
who understands perfectly
"Sit," "Shake," "Heel,"
"Stay," "No," "Come here,"
"Get your toy," "Off the bed,"
"Walk," "Haircut,"
and of course,
"Who did this?"
has an apricot pit of a brain.
Size should not matter.
Yet most of us admit,
if only to ourselves,
that it most certainly does.

★

As a child,
I suffered nightmares.
Unable to sleep,
I would hunch
on the edge of the bed
rubbing my thumb
and index finger,
a cure for anxiety
taught to me
by my mother.
With eyelids slammed shut,
the distance I felt between
the rows of fingerprints
seemed extraordinary,
the ridges and valleys

marvelous.
Years later,
examining
a flap of dead skin
under a microscope,
I saw that this was true,
and I slept much better.

★

Like my father and mother
before me,
my wife and I
talk about size:
of fingers, toes, ear lobes,
bellies, chins, noses.
Of newborns.
The x-ray raised up
to the ceiling bulb
reveals an empty space,
shapeless almost.
I want to say
it is the size of something,
bigger than this,
smaller than that.
Except,
I do not know
how to figure this.
It is dwarfed by comparison
to my immeasurable
longing and sadness.

WALKING THE DOGS

The dogs were like little boys tonight,
too energetic, and ran far across the meadow
into the dark, away from the arched lamps

lining the cracked paths, only stopping
or glancing back when we were out of reach.
The moon above was a sliver, too thin

to do anything but hang, and if it, too,
had a soul, then on this night at the end
of summer in New York, I could say

the moon was like a young girl, sad
and innocent, or a mother, alone and graying.
I have finally come to like this world,

even the artificial light gleaming on the horizon,
and the faint noise of barges in the distance
remind me of driftwood in Michigan.

When we called out their names, the dogs
hurried back. Hunched on their hind legs, they waited
for us to hook their leashes, to praise them,

to act as if nothing else in the universe mattered,
nothing except an adoration that seems
to have been born with creation itself.

These dogs, too, whose souls are as bright,
or dark, as my own, if only for one night
ignored instinct and refused to howl at the moon.

DOG POEM

My dog and I do not
resemble each other.
His eyelids do not droop.
My breath is considerably
fresher, and though hair
covers his entire face,
it is difficult to tell
one way or the other
if he has a unibrow.

So much has been written
about dogs, I have left mine
out of poems. Yet
I am grateful that he waits
for me when I write late at night,
and on more than one occasion
he stood on his hind legs,
pawed at my hands,
and saved me from ruining
a perfectly good metaphor.

Last night a muted howl
like that of a man trying, but failing,
to keep his misery to himself
roused me from sleep.
For a brief moment
I thought my dog was dying.
His body curled inward
like a fetus in the womb.
His nose twitched. Nervously,
I waited until I saw his chest
rise and fall. I sighed
in relief and imagined him
chasing a fire engine in his dreams.

I love this creature, who
no matter how much I may wish
will never know more than
my affection and my disapproval.

In that quiet darkness, I knew
this was more than enough,
both for my dog and for me.

FORGIVENESS

Now, at 6:59 A.M., one minute
before the alarm clock's wake-up,
a startling noise after all these years,
I'm wondering about forgiveness.
I smell the sweet odor
against my chin of Sweetpea's breath,
he the Siamese my wife found
abandoned at a real estate office,
who hunts fledgling sparrows,
frogs, lizards, and playfully
murders crickets and June bugs.
He who was struck by a vehicle
and waited for us to discover him
curled like a fetus on the doormat,
and he who last night, for seemingly
no good reason whatsoever,
burst into a frenzy, fiercely
clawed my arm, and drew blood.
Now, with seconds before
the lull in the house is replaced
by the clamor of wakefulness,
I hesitate to switch off the alarm
so not to disturb the peace
he has settled into on my chest.
I'm wondering if there is such a thing
as forgiveness, if it descended upon me
while I slept, unaware of its lurking
in the darkness of these rooms,
if it is possible not only to forgive
but also to cast past hurts
out of memory. Without hesitation,
the alarm goes off, and my cat's ears
twitch. But that's all, nothing else.
And maybe because I expect this,
I let it go, incessantly, until my wife
nudges me with her elbow, and the cat,
reluctantly, finds comfort somewhere else.

THE SADNESS OF OTHERS

A week ago, my father
unpacked his boxes
in another country, a place
so much unlike here.
His home is again
his homeland. His home—
not mine, nor my sister's,
who after watching his plane
disappear into a cloudless sky
drove forty miles to our mother.
She, our mother,
is a headstone
in a flat cemetery
behind the interstate. She,
my sister,
like my mother, is finally alone.
And I am so far away,
unable to distinguish
which I love more,
her or her sadness.
Thinking of this,
I cannot help
but wonder what happened
to the stray cat
I used to feed, the thin one
I always look for
first thing in the morning
after a long night's sleep.

MY BEST DAYS

At school,
all my students showed up,
and the day before,
listening to thirty-eight
minutes of Bach,
some dozed, some yawned,
others tapped their fingertips,
but none of them walked out
or complained.
Driving home,
I made every traffic light.
At the supermarket,
pumpkins were two for four dollars
and the check-out lines
moved quickly.
The dogs greeted me
at the fence,
and the cat, too.
None of them shit in the house.
My wife arrived
earlier than expected
and we made dinner
together—
rice, beans, chicken, salad.
I was not bored
reading student papers.
I enjoyed
the television program
I watched,
and not once
did the telephone ring.
During the night,
I slept fitfully,
woke several times,
and though I suffered nightmares,
I could not remember them
in the morning.
My best days are now.
Always have been.

JOB INTERVIEW

He drew a line across the page
and asked where I expected to be
five years from here. Honestly,
I had no clue. And I can admit now,
without shame or remorse,
that it's always been easier
for me to go back.
I was still young five years ago,
drank more, smoked less,
had significantly more teeth.
Yet my first wife had left me
for a man with a thin nose,
and there was also my mother.
Could I admit that when she stopped
visiting my dreams, I gave up
on the future and because of this
was sleeping much better?
Outside the world was bright
under the afternoon sun. Except,
the forecast called for rain.
I wondered if it mattered whether
the downpour would come,
which it did, or that we sat
with our hands folded at a table
that would outlast us both.
He asked me once more.
As he stared past me, I breathed
deeply and tried not to blink.
And a grin broke across his face,
like a crack in the sidewalk
patiently waiting for someone
to stumble and fall.

FAMILY REUNIONS

We didn't do them.
Not in the fashion of those
scattered groups
from this and that state,
armed with AAA maps
and pots of beans,
tuna casseroles,
family t-shirts,
gossip, good and bad,
who joined together
and toasted each other,
congratulated themselves
on a job well done—
presumably
the continuance
of the clan—
and who,
for at least a single afternoon,
set aside their ill will
and even,
should they be lucky,
no longer bore each other
any more harm or malice.
We didn't do that.
For one, we lived
in close proximity—
a dozen aunts and uncles,
their husbands and wives,
and their progeny
far too many to count.
Yet make no mistake,
a picnic once a year
would have forced
brother against brother
to sit face to face
once too often.
And they would have
wished upon themselves
any one of the following calamities:

ticks, plagues,
weight gain,
early gray hair,
sudden baldness,
facial warts, migraines,
kidney stones,
enlarged prostates,
tax audits, job loss,
unwanted pregnancies,
illegitimate offspring—
who might be in attendance—
and, of course,
an early demise.
And not necessarily
in that order.
We did not bother with reunions.
No need to plan ahead,
to RSVP, to book
hotel reservations.
Besides, we had funerals,
which consigned us
to each other
regularly enough.
There, we paid our respects,
due or not.

TRAFFIC

At rush hour, I sit in traffic,
surrounded by candidates,
those, including myself,
who might be
next in line—not for the light
at the intersection,
though I suppose a light
at an unearthly crossroad
is a reasonable possibility.
What I mean, of course,
is what might become of us:
the two workers
in the pickup truck
listening to the radio,
the young woman
directly ahead
who brakes for animals,
the couple reading a map
in the coupe with out-of-state plates,
or me, shifting uncomfortably
in my seat, imagining
the mess that would result
if one of the planes soaring
overhead suddenly
nose-dives onto
this stretch of road
that we're all on.
Isn't it like that?
Even the long, drawn-out deaths
come to an end
just like that.
I could gesture
to the cab driver
on my left
to roll down his window,
to say a word
on the off chance
that he is the last person
with whom I speak.

But he is already
agitated enough,
stuck here, no hire
clicking away the minutes,
and somewhere ahead of us,
something is keeping us
from moving forward.
He keeps arching
his head over the dashboard
to figure out
what's holding us back,
and because of this,
I keep it to myself—
the uncertainty,
above all else,
is what troubles him most.

HERE IT IS

Here it is, at daybreak, again, one square foot,
its yellowish paint half darkened, its surface

marred by gum, spilled soda pop, spit. The rest
muffled by footsteps. It's mine for as long as it takes,

until the transfer to Queens thrusts the smell
of urine, rat and human, and pours it onto the platform.

Five minutes maybe, or an hour during this period
of heightened security. Today, so much like

yesterday, so much unlike before, I slope my head
to see lights beaming against the tiled walls,

looming on the tracks. I bend forward to notice
the scurry of mice, their ears and feet my measuring tools.

Today, again, I ignore the pleas of a man who
might be hunched over, proud. I ignore the restless

who speculate global losses, and I ignore
the stories and believe the headlines.

"Exact Punishment for Evil."
"A Tough City Swept by Anger."

One square foot in lower Manhattan costs more
than the surgery doctors performed on my father's

second wife, more than the headstone purchased
five years prior for his first. Here,

temporary property is sold cheap, a dollar fifty
for as long as it takes, and among strangers,

without bargaining, names are sold cheaply,
lives are exchanged as commodities. Now, I am

inches from the edge, from the obituaries
if someone wishes. I am not like them. My eyes, nose,

color fit the wrong description. The train will arrive.
Step back. My safety depends upon theirs.

MORE THAN WE DARED

They were convinced that our scent
attracted flies, that the taxi cabs

driven by our uncles in New York
reeked of arm pits, that we never

used the deodorant sticks stocked
in our grocery stores. When they saw

two or more of us in a car, they knew
there'd be trouble. They honked,

told us to "Go home." They never
called us by the names

our mothers and fathers heard
echoed in their dreams. Instead,

they shouted "Camel Jockey,"
"Sand Nigger," "Dirty Mud Dweller."

We married first cousins.
We feared pork.

We beat our sisters, mothers,
and wives. The nuns in grade school

said we worshipped the Devil.
They nicknamed us Mike and Abe

and Charlie because Mohammed
and Abdul and Kahlil were too hard

to pronounce. But they loved
our food—hummus, tabouli, shawarma.

They waited in lines to eat it,
drove miles on lunch breaks

to find it, begged our mothers
for the recipes. They could not

get enough of the taste.
Even when they cleared their throats

and spit on the sidewalks
to imitate the language we spoke,

they wanted more,
more than we dared to give.

THE PRICE OF TOMATOES

The cardboard sign reads
"$1.99 each."

Granted, they're blood red,
firm, smell like my mother's garden.

Yet I cannot figure out
the price of these tomatoes.

I hold one up
under the long fluorescent bulbs

and remember the afternoon
when my mother, pruning

vines while on her knees
in the dirt, received news from Lebanon

about her father's shrinking stomach.
Plucked, left in the sun,

the fruits burst, their seeds
festered on the cracked earth

like tiny cancers.
"Israeli tomatoes,"

the grocer explains.
I leave the bag on the counter.

My grandfather, whose stomach
shrank to almost nothing,

smaller than a clenched fist,
wanted only clean water,

but the soldier,
who spoke Hebrew and Arabic,

refused. Instead,
he washed his shoes,

which were dirty, same as these
bright, shiny tomatoes

that cost so much.

DOWNTOWN

I wanted the #6 train
to sweep through the station,
feel itself weighing down the rails,
see the emptiness ahead
before screeching to a halt,
and somehow,
conscious of its burden,
to let me be—
a shadow lengthening
across the platform.

Everything about this
seemed so much like failure:
the hulking mass
reduced to a crawl,
the wrenching screams of rust
against rust—not deafening,
not impressive at all,
only a presence.

I asked for nothing more
than the rats scurrying
under the tracks would have
had they the power of speech.
Even more, I wanted a cigarette,
but my empty hard pack
I'd already crushed
and heaved into a metal trash can.

Waiting for the transfer,
I imagined smoking,
the curlicues above my head
sifting through the steel grates
to the sidewalks above
where the leaves of a ginkgo
chained to a concrete block
hung like flags
drooped in defeat.

WINTER, DETROIT

Even while you sit there, unmovable,
You have begun to vanish. And it does not matter.
    —Donald Justice

There is only the muffled clank
of radiators. Everything else
is remote and quiet.
The street lamps that summon moths,
the shingled rooftops and the birch
all slope toward a long silence.
He knows this house will outlast him,
as it did his wife.

He unclogs the eaves trough,
cranks up the converted steam boiler,
measures out fifteen yards
of weatherproofing strips
for the attic and basement cellar,
and stirs three paint cans
for the smoke stains on the ceilings.

Under a single bulb grimed with dust,
he lights a Chesterfield
and holds the matchstick
between his thumb and index finger.
Slowly, a column of smoke
becomes invisible. All afternoon
he had listened for footsteps. Now
he decides to drive to the cemetery.
Gently, he closes the door behind him
as if he were never coming back,
and already these rooms are becoming empty
but no emptier for his absence.

THERE WERE THE USUAL REASONS

What about the mother
who swallowed tranquilizers

at her son's funeral,
not for pain

but for disbelief,
the one who sealed her sorrow

in a childproof bottle
and swears to this day

that she has forgotten
the origin of her pain?

FALLING OFF THE BRIDGE

The emergency room nurse asked if I suspected
that my friend's fall, thirty feet backwards
off a bridge, had been more than an accident.

I had known him long enough to say,
"He's a drunken idiot." But when I said this,
I admitted with even more certainty, "I don't know."

For a whole year he had waited for his mother
to die, watching her body disappear day by day
until she weighed almost nothing.

All I could think is what he must have looked like
to the crows perched on the telephone wires,
his featherless arms flapping, flapping, falling down.

His skull fractured in two places, his femur
smashed like a bag of ice. The nurse told me
to go home. Instead, I waited and waited.

ENGLISH 101

after John Brehm

When I was teaching "America"
at a community college in Warren,
a suburb of Detroit,
my freshmen admitted
that they had never
heard of Allen Ginsberg.
"Okay," I said. "Let's talk
about Whitman first."
From the back seats,
a young woman raised her hand
and asked, "Who's he?"
Another in the same row
added with confidence,
"He's a writer . . . or something."
I sighed. He was a poet,
I told them, and then I asked
reluctantly, "Do you remember
Dead Poets Society?"
The first student's eyes
widened and she blurted out,
"He wrote *carpe diem!*"
I inhaled deeply
and remembered my mother,
a schoolteacher
until she died,
who was inclined
to count backwards from ten
when she wanted to avoid
embarrassing her first-graders.

Good God, I thought.
If I quiz them on Eminem
or *American Idol*, their pens will
run out of ink. And do I always
have to refer to Hollywood?
"Class, here's the story.
Shakespeare composed sonnets

for Gwyneth Paltrow,
and he was awarded
the highest honor for his achievement,
an Oscar. And you know how
in *Pulp Fiction* a Big Mac
is le Big Mac? See,
in ancient Greece, Homer
Simpson was blind
and liked to rant and rave
about monsters with one eye—
imagine a donut.
Oh, by the way,
all poems rhyme;
the movie is always better
than the book; and if
the poem is not in English,
don't waste your time.
Most important,
the more a poet uses the word 'love,'
the better . . . ."

Of course, I didn't say that.
For twenty years, my mother
woke at six o'clock,
brewed coffee, smoked a cigarette,
and stepped through the doors—
her shoulders
slightly drooped,
her back slouched
as if anticipating a heavy weight—
without complaining,
utterly gratified
to face the dumb questions,
the obvious remarks,
the generous ignorance.
She knew that otherwise
she'd cheat them.
I knew it, too.
I could have betrayed them,

given a simple answer
to a simple question.
Yet there was an hour left.
Rain drizzled on the quad.
A piece of chalk rested on my desk.
And they were waiting for me,
to teach, to share with them,
to give up what was mine
and what, if willing enough,
they could make their own.

THE LITURGY OF RAIN

after William Stafford

I remember a sudden downpour,
darkness coming fast
over the river,
the city concealed,
the vanishing point on the horizon
too blurred to say this or that about.
But a mile away,
my father's Buick was dry,
the Turtle Wax finish
gleaming in the bright light of summer.

Even the rain neglects us.
But that is the liturgy of rain—
always ambivalent, indifferent, inchoate.
And when we slip away from each other
like shirts from a clothesline pulley,
we return to this unmistakable uncertainty.
Finally, rain gives the blessing.

TO MY EX-WIFE

The shades were drawn,
a dog barked outside,
and my eyelids sank.
When I woke,
suddenly,
at half past midnight,
I knew I had forgiven you.
I was alone,
half a year since
our marriage,
six hundred miles
from the table
we sat across
where you said we had
lost our way
and I begged you
to find it again.

If there was a reason
for why now,
why like this,
it was lost
and didn't matter anymore.
Instead,
the droop of your shoulders,
your tedious breathing,
the exact time
you took to walk the hallway
never to return the same—
these mattered.

We'd become,
without realizing it,
so much unlike
the way we were.
And once more,
I sat stiff,
the moon whitened,
and I found myself

wholly changed
from one moment to the next,
and nothing but nothing
could explain.

PAPERWEIGHT

A half globe, see-through,
crystal with felt tip bottom.
Inside, a painted monkey,
curious in an overstuffed chair,
eyeing a pair of spectacles.
Of course, its feet rest
on a book of maps—
weighing down the world,
doing its job.
I never use it for papers.
Same as the antique typewriter
with the jammed *e*
and the camera without a shutter,
this paperweight is a reminder
more than a tool.
I see it and think of my wife,
far away as the countries
etched in yellow and blue,
out of reach as the illustration
behind this heavy glass.

THE MARRIED COUPLE'S ORCHIDS

Three have leaves
like tongues of German Shepherds.
Ceramic god-heads surround
the one whose calyxes
resemble flattened watermelons—
the cat perches on the bark chips
to taste its brittle roots.
Opposite the vacant bedroom,
the oldest. It wants round-the-clock shade,
refuses the most water.
All have blossomed,
their petals a multitude
of delicate insect wings,
flesh like mysterious maps.
Except one.
Not a single petal since their marriage.
This, their talked about, their set-aside,
the one that reminds them
of their patience, their yearning,
their life together.

UNFINISHED BUSINESS

My father refused to donate
her clothes to the Salvation Army.
The long-sleeve shirt
she had tossed
into the laundry basket
the morning she died,
he hung in their bedroom closet:
the lingering smell of her perfume
a reminder in case he forgets.
Her shoes are still
at the bottom of the stairwell.
Her purse, everything in it,
remains undisturbed
behind the dresser:
the expired driver's license,
grade school photographs
of my sister and me,
a disposable lighter,
butterscotch drops,
and the keys to her Ford,
which he has left parked at the curb
for the last two years.

REACQUAINTANCE

after Jane Kenyon

The thermometer reads 102.
I lumber to the kitchen,
pour honey into boiling water,
add tea leaves, and stir in
the juice of a lemon—
my mother's flu remedy.
I bring the cup to my mouth,
and smelling it, I remember
the late nights of coughing,
of fevers, of cold sweats,
how I begged not to taste,
how she sipped from it,
cajoling me to drink.
I swallow the elixir,
gagging, and I grieve for her now
as if it were the day she died.

TO MY MOTHER ON THE OCCASION OF THE FIFTH YEAR OF HER DEATH

If I pledge to lie down
with a single woman
until death or some other calamity
tears us apart,
it will be for the second time.
Forgive me if on that day
I refuse to weep.
There are worse things.
My taxes, for instance,
require an accountant
though not on account of my income.
My teeth are ruined, too,
and the laziness I am famous for
will guarantee the swelling
I noticed three years ago
to threaten malignancy.
There are worse things.
The landlord may discover
that he can no longer
remain indifferent
to the noise of my footsteps,
and the keys that unlock
what I keep hidden
will become useless.
Or worse, my pocket watch,
which my students rely on
more than I do,
may stop ticking, and everyone
falls into a coma.
Once a year I try to visit
your grave. On the last trip,
I did not bring peonies.
My pockets were empty.
And the year prior to that
I drove downtown instead,
amused myself with a drunk
bent on teaching me proper posture.
This year, I disconnected
the phone lines

and erased the messages
from my father and sister,
who mourn openly
and without regret.
Next year I may in fact
admit that I have never understood
the loneliness of others
and that there is
an end to dying.
There are worse things.
My mother,
there are worse things
that I could wish for
than to wake late
in the afternoon
only to realize I have been
motherless this long,
and each day is still
another to come.

BLACK EARTH

After my mother died,
gravediggers broke and turned the ground

with a mechanical plow.
The thaw came and the stiff thatch

loosened, and before grass burst through,
a marker etched with her name

laid into a plotted square.
When it rains, the dirt on its edges

sinks, spills over, and the letters
that belong to her name

become crusted with black dirt.
I know this because my father told me.

After every storm, he drives
to the graveyard, rubs his fingers

between the cracks and grooves,
returns with black earth under his nails.

CHANGING THE SUBJECT

Yesterday,
you were
dead
exactly
seven years.
Unlike
before,
I did not cry,
and for
only a brief
moment,
I closed
my eyes
to imagine
you
otherwise.
On
this
anniversary,
I lectured
about
how incidents
change
people,
how we can
never
go back
once we have
moved
forward.
I wanted
to use
your death
as an example.
I hesitated.
I studied
the wall clock.
I stepped
forward

and,
forgive me,
I changed
the subject.

THE RAIN

Outside. Always looking outside.
The bare bulb hanging loosely
under the awning
attracting locusts.
By next week,
only their shells
will cling to the wood siding.
And the leaves, too, will drift away.
Regardless, the neighbor,
whose mailbox is a painted landscape
that exists only
in the histories of nostalgia,
will sweep her broom
across a clean porch.
There is a moon, too.
The crescent blurred
by clouds and, perhaps,
by my poor vision.
Stars, obviously,
though faint. Silence?
This would not be midnight
if not for the quiet.
Here, in the middle of Texas,
so far from where my mother was born,
from where she was buried.
Except, the chirping of a bird
whose name I do not know.
The noise, when I first heard it,
like a girl crying.
But no other disturbances.
No street lamps flickering,
no traffic.
If I holler out, the old woman
whose mailbox I love
will call the police.
This unnerving calm.
This, eight years since she died.
And the rain. I forget there was the rain,
overwhelming everything entirely.

THE LAST THING

I am watching the animals.
The cat perched
on the fence,
the dogs gnawing branches
fallen from pecan trees,
and a moth—
what it does
so seemingly without effort,
I cannot know.

So. This is how it begins.

1995
Germany, Caroline Finkelstein
Housekeeping in a Dream, Laura Kasischke
About Distance, Gregory Djanikian
Wind of the White Dresses, Mekeel McBride
Above the Tree Line, Kathy Mangan
In the Country of Elegies, T. Alan Broughton
Scenes from the Light Years, Anne C. Bromley
Quartet, Angela Ball
Rorschach Test, Franz Wright

1996
Back Roads, Patricia Henley
Dyer's Thistle, Peter Balakian
Beckon, Gillian Conoley
The Parable of Fire, James Reiss
Cold Pluto, Mary Ruefle
Orders of Affection, Arthur Smith
Colander, Michael McFee

1997
Growing Darkness, Growing Light, Jean Valentine
Selected Poems, 1965-1995, Michael Dennis Browne
Your Rightful Childhood: New and Selected Poems, Paula Rankin
Headlands: New and Selected Poems, Jay Meek
Soul Train, Allison Joseph
The Autobiography of a Jukebox, Cornelius Eady
The Patience of the Cloud Photographer, Elizabeth Holmes
Madly in Love, Aliki Barnstone
An Octave Above Thunder: New and Selected Poems, Carol Muske

1998
Yesterday Had a Man In It, Leslie Adrienne Miller
Definition of the Soul, John Skoyles
Dithyrambs, Richard Katrovas
Postal Routes, Elizabeth Kirschner
The Blue Salvages, Wayne Dodd

The Joy Addict, James Harms
Clemency and Other Poems, Colette Inez
Scattering the Ashes, Jeff Friedman
Sacred Conversations, Peter Cooley
Life Among the Trolls, Maura Stanton

1999
Justice, Caroline Finkelstein
Edge of House, Dzvinia Orlowsky
A Thousand Friends of Rain: New and Selected Poems, 1976-1998,
      Kim Stafford
The Devil's Child, Fleda Brown Jackson
World as Dictionary, Jesse Lee Kercheval
Vereda Tropical, Ricardo Pau-Llosa
The Museum of the Revolution, Angela Ball
Our Master Plan, Dara Wier

2000
Small Boat with Oars of Different Size, Thom Ward
Post Meridian, Mary Ruefle
Hierarchies of Rue, Roger Sauls
Constant Longing, Dennis Sampson
Mortal Education, Joyce Peseroff
How Things Are, James Richardson
Years Later, Gregory Djanikian
On the Waterbed They Sank to Their Own Levels, Sarah Rosenblatt
Blue Jesus, Jim Daniels
Winter Morning Walks: 100 Postcards to Jim Harrison, Ted Kooser

2001
The Deepest Part of the River, Mekeel McBride
The Origin of Green, T. Alan Broughton
Day Moon, Jon Anderson
Glacier Wine, Maura Stanton
Earthly, Michael McFee
Lovers in the Used World, Gillian Conoley
Sex Lives of the Poor and Obscure, David Schloss

Voyages in English, Dara Wier
Quarters, James Harms
Mastodon, 80% Complete, Jonathan Johnson
Ten Thousand Good Mornings, James Reiss
The World's Last Night, Margot Schilpp

2002
Among the Musk Ox People, Mary Ruefle
The Memphis Letters, Jay Meek
What it Wasn't, Laura Kasischke
The Finger Bone, Kevin Prufer
The Late World, Arthur Smith
Slow Risen Among the Smoke Trees, Elizabeth Kirschner
Keeping Time, Suzanne Cleary
Astronaut, Brian Henry

2003
Imitation of Life, Allison Joseph
A Place Made of Starlight, Peter Cooley
The Mastery Impulse, Ricardo Pau-Llosa
Except for One Obscene Brushstroke, Dzvinia Orlowsky
Taking Down the Angel, Jeff Friedman
Casino of the Sun, Jerry Williams
Trouble, Mary Baine Campbell
Lives of Water, John Hoppenthaler

2004
Freeways and Aqueducts, James Harms
Tristimania, Mary Ruefle
Prague Winter, Richard Katrovas
Venus Examines Her Breast, Maureen Seaton
Trains in Winter, Jay Meek
The Women Who Loved Elvis All Their Lives, Fleda Brown
The Chronic Liar Buys a Canary, Elizabeth Edwards
Various Orbits, Thom Ward

2005

Laws of My Nature, Margot Schilpp
Things I Can't Tell You, Michael Dennis Browne
Renovation, Jeffrey Thomson
Sleeping Woman, Herbert Scott
Blindsight, Carol Hamilton
Fallen from a Chariot, Kevin Prufer
Needlegrass, Dennis Sampson
Bent to the Earth, Blas Manuel De Luna

2006

Burn the Field, Amy Beeder
Dog Star Delicatessen: New and Selected Poems 1979-2006,
      Mekeel McBride
The Sadness of Others, Hayan Charara
A Grammar to Waking, Nancy Eimers
Shinemaster, Michael McFee
Eastern Mountain Time, Joyce Peseroff
Dragging the Lake, Robert Thomas